Copyright © 2020 Nigel Gordo

All rights reserved

The characters and events portrayed in this book are fictitious. Any similarity to real persons, living or dead, is coincidental and not intended by the author.

No part of this book may be reproduced, or stored in a retrieval system, or transmitted in any form or by any means, electronic, mechanical, photocopying, recording, or otherwise, without express written permission of the publisher.

ISBN: 9798577382537
Imprint: Independently published

Cover design by: Art Painter
Library of Congress Control Number: 2018675309
Printed in the United States of America

CONTENTS

Copyright	
David Beckham	3
Ian Holloway	5
Paul Gascoigne – Gazza	7
Brian Clough	9
Wayne Rooney	11
Jose Mourinho	13
Sir Alex Ferguson	16
Zlatan Ibrahimovic	18
Arsene Wenger	21
Diego Maradona	23
Gary Lineker	25
Sir Bobby Robson	27
Mario Balotelli	29
Ally McCoist	31
Gianluca Vialli	32
Graham Taylor	34
Charlie Nicholas	36
Stan Collymore	37
Alan Brazil	38
Eric Cantona	40

Roy Keane	42
Chris Kamara	45
Paul Merson	47
Sam Allardyce	49
Glenn Hoddle	51
Jack Charlton	53
Gary Neville	55
Michael Owen	57
Graeme Souness	59
Ron Atkinson	61
Andy Gray	65
Kevin Keegan	67
George Best	70
Andrea Pirlo	73
Joey Barton	75
Vinnie Jones	77
Harry Redknapp	79
Books By This Author	83

World's Funniest Football Quotes

By

Nigel Gordon-Johnson

NIGEL GORDON-JOHNSON

If you are like me then you love football. The skill and grace of a Johan Cruff, Diego Maradona or Lionel Messi. The ecstasy of that great victory for your team or country. And the agony of defeat or relegation after a hard-fought campaign. Just that alone makes football the world's greatest sport.

But the icing on the cake is that footballers tend not to think too much before speaking. This has given us some of the funniest quotes of all time.

I have put together some of my favourite players and managers from around the world and my favourite funny quotes.

I hope that you find these as funny as I did writing them in this book. Some real classics that will have you in stitches!

Enjoy!

DAVID BECKHAM

What better place to start than with Captain Golden Balls himself. Just like Rodney on Only Fools & Horses, David Beckham got a couple of GCSE's. And you can clearly see why. Becks is the Gold Standard when it comes to funny football quotes.

I definitely want Brooklyn to be christened, but I don't know into what religion yet - David Beckham

Interviewer: **Would it be fair to describe you as a volatile player?**

David Beckham: **Well, I can play in the centre, on the right and occasionally on the left side**

Alex Ferguson is the best manager I've ever had at this level. Well, he's the only manager I've actually had at this level. But he's the best manager I've ever had – David Beckham

My parents have been there for me, ever since I was about seven – David Beckham

I remember so clearly us going into hospital so Victoria could have Brooklyn. I was eating a Lion bar at the time – David Beckham

Pele was a complete player. I didn't see him live obviously, because I wasn't born – David Beckham

NIGEL GORDON-JOHNSON

I always wanted to be a hairdresser – David Beckham

I think I've lost a lot of my gay fans to Gavin Henson. It's a shame because I really love them – David Beckham

I've always tended to go for the tighter, smaller trunks. I don't know why – David Beckham

We (Victoria & Becks) like to lock the doors at night and wander around naked – David Beckham

IAN HOLLOWAY

The most famous Bristolian since Bananarama and Noel Edmonds. Banksy too hails from Bristol and it's a well-known fact that Ian Holloway and Banksy have never been seen together in the same place. There again no one has ever seen Banksy anywhere. Ian Holloway is definitely the Banksy of funny football quotes.

To put it in gentlemen's terms. If you've been for a night out and you're looking for a young lady and you pull one, you've done what you set out to do. We didn't look our best today, but we pulled. Some weeks the lady is good looking and some weeks she's not. Our performance today would have been not the best-looking bird, but at least we got her in the taxi. She may not have been the best-looking lady we ended up taking home, but it was still very pleasant and very nice, so thanks very much and let's have coffee – Ian Holloway

I couldn't be more chuffed if I were a badger at the start of the mating season – Ian Holloway

I love Blackpool. We're very similar. We both look better in the dark – Ian Holloway

Every dog has its day and today is woof day! Today I just want to bark – Ian Holloway

In the first half we were like the Dog and Duck, in the second half like Real Madrid. We can't go on like that. At full-time I was like an irritated Jack Russell! – Ian Holloway

If you're a burglar, it's no good poncing about outside somebody's house, looking good with your swag bag ready. Just get in there, burgle them and come out. I don't advocate that obviously. It's just an analogy – Ian Holloway

There was a time in the second half when I took my heart off my sleeve and put it in my mouth – Ian Holloway

We're like a bad tea-bag – we never stay in the cup that long – Ian Holloway

I watched Arsenal in the Champions League the other week, playing some of the best football I've ever seen and yet they couldn't have scored in a brothel with two grand in their pockets – Ian Holloway

Apparently, it's my fault that the Titanic sank – Ian Holloway

PAUL GASCOIGNE – GAZZA

Arguably England's greatest ever footballer with supreme skills but mostly remembered fondly by the nation for his tears at the 1990 World Cup and his friendship with Jimmy Five Bellies. Gazza's love of kebabs and practical jokes are world renowned.

I've had 14 bookings this season; eight of which were my fault, but seven of which were disputable - Paul Gascoigne

I never make predictions and I never will – Paul Gascoigne

What is the world coming to when you get a red card and get fined two weeks' wages for calling a grown man a w##ker? – Paul Gascoigne

I'll tell you the truth; I had a double brandy before the game but, before, it used to be four bottles of whisky. Not anymore. I was fine. I had a glass of wine after the game. But it was just a mouthful – Paul Gascoigne

I'll tell you what my real dream is. I mean my absolute number one dream that will mean I die a happy man if it happens. I want to see a UFO. They're real. I don't care if you look at me like that. UFO's are a definite fact and I've got to see one soon – Paul Gascoigne

I got eight O-levels at school...zero in every subject – Paul Gascoigne

Daft as a brush? I'm daft, but I'm not daft as a brush! – Paul Gascoigne

The Chairman wants to sack me, but I said I will never walk away from Kettering Town and I will fight all the way. I am now looking to buy the football club – Paul Gascoigne

I didn't know Walter Smith, but I knew he must be Scottish because I saw him carrying big discount cases of lager back from the supermarket – Paul Gascoigne

He really squeezed them so hard. Honestly, I thought I'd lost my family allowance – Paul Gascoigne on his infamous altercation with Vinnie Jones

BRIAN CLOUGH

Cloughie only played for three clubs. Middlesbrough, Sunderland and the mighty Billingham Synthonia. But it was for his great managerial career and trophy winning funny quotes that he is more famous for. The greatest manager England never had.

When I go, God's going to have to give up his favourite chair – Brian Clough

The River Trent is lovely, I know because I have walked on it for 18 years – Brian Clough

I'm loath to confess they could be as good as us. They are brilliant. It sticks in the craw a little bit because nobody likes Arsenal! Of course there's a Frenchman in charge, Wenger, and not many English people like Frenchmen. He is a top, top manager - Brian Clough on Arsenal beating Nottingham Forest's 42 games unbeaten

Resignations are for prime ministers and those caught with their trousers down, not for me - Brian Clough

I wouldn't say I was the best manager in the business. But I was in the top one – Brian Clough

We talk about it for 20 minutes and then we decide I was right -

NIGEL GORDON-JOHNSON

Brian Clough

I only ever hit Roy the once. He got up so I couldn't have hit him very hard - Brian Clough on his managerial style with Roy Keane

Players lose you games, not tactics. There's so much crap talked about tactics by people who barely know how to win at dominoes - Brian Clough

If the BBC ran a Crap Decision of the Month competition on Match of the Day, I'd walk it – Brian Clough after Nottingham Forest were relegated

If any one of my players isn't interfering with play, they're not getting paid – Brian Clough

WAYNE ROONEY

Wayne comes from Liverpool and is England's youngest ever goal scorer. Wayne Rooney also holds the dubious distinction of being the most red carded player for England. An honour he shares with our hero David Beckham.

Just to confirm to all my followers I have had a hair transplant. I was going bald at 25 why not – Wayne Rooney

Nice to see your home fans boo you. That's what loyal support is – Wayne Rooney

I listen to 50 Cent, Jay-Z, Stereophonics, Arctic Monkeys; also the musical Oliver – I can sing every tune – Wayne Rooney

I don't normally cook, but if I did it probably would be beans, sausage, bacon and eggs. I never really get to eat that to be honest – Wayne Rooney

I am mentally strong – Wayne Rooney

I'm proud I'm English and I'm passionate about my country – Wayne Rooney

I'm only a human being – Wayne Rooney

Part of my preparation is I go and ask the kit man what colour we're wearing - if it's red top, white shorts, white socks or black socks. Then I lie in bed the night before the game and visualise myself scoring goals or doing well – Wayne Rooney

Unlike others who have been caught swearing on camera, I apologised immediately. And yet I am the only person banned for swearing. That doesn't seem right – Wayne Rooney

I don't think I look up to any players. Obviously you respect everyone – Wayne Rooney

JOSE MOURINHO

Plain and simple......The Special One

Please do not call me arrogant because what I say is true. I'm European champion. I'm not one out of the bottle, I think I'm a special one – Jose Mourinho

Young players are like melons. Only when you open and taste the melon are you 100% sure that the melon is good – Jose Mourinho

You may as well put a cow in the middle of the pitch, walking. And then stop the game because there was a cow – Jose Mourinho

Fear is not a word in my football dictionary – Jose Mourinho

At the moment, we cannot walk from the bed to the toilet without breaking a leg – Jose Mourinho

I want to push the young players on my team to have a proper haircut, not the Rastafarian or the others they have – Jose Mourinho

It's like having a blanket that is too small for the bed. You pull the blanket up to keep your chest warm and your feet stick out. I cannot buy a bigger blanket because the supermarket is closed. But the blanket is made of cashmere – Jose Mourinho

We have top players and, sorry if I'm arrogant, we have a top manager – Jose Mourinho

I have a problem, which is I'm getting better at everything related to my job since I started – Jose Mourinho

It's not important how we play. If you have a Ferrari and I have a small car, to beat you in a race I have to break your wheel or put sugar in your tank – Jose Mourinho

I would rather play with 10 men than wait for a player who is late for the bus – Jose Mourinho

Look, I'm a coach, I'm not Harry Potter. He is magical, but in reality, there is no magic. Magic is fiction and football is real – Jose Mourinho

If they made a film of my life, I think they should get George Clooney to play me. He's a fantastic actor and my wife thinks he would be ideal – Jose Mourinho

We are a little horse. A horse that still needs milk and to learn how to jump – Jose Mourinho

Can Messi be suspended for acting? Barcelona is a cultural city with many great theatres and this boy has learned very well. He's learned play-acting – Jose Mourinho

Every time I play Pep [Guardiola] I end up with 10 men. It must be some sort of UEFA rule – Jose Mourinho

We don't have A, B, C, D, E, F and G - but we do have L, M, N, S, O, P –

Jose Mourinho

Sometimes you see beautiful people with no brains. Sometimes you have ugly people who are intelligent, like scientists – Jose Mourinho

If Roman Abramovich helped me out in training we would be bottom of the league and if I had to work in his world of big business, we would be bankrupt – Jose Mourinho

When you enjoy what you do, you don't lose your hair, and Guardiola is bald. He doesn't enjoy football – Jose Mourinho

My wife is in Portugal with the dog. The dog is with my wife so the city of London is safe, the big threat is away – Jose Mourinho

One day somebody will punch you – Jose Mourinho

SIR ALEX FERGUSON

He was the Gaffer. Took over Manchester United when they were pretty average and was just one game away from getting the sack. The rest is history. Feared in the dressing room. Feared in the press room. Feared on the side-lines. Feared everywhere basically.

You can't applaud a referee – Alex Ferguson

I remember the first time I saw him. He was 13 and just floated over the ground like a cocker spaniel chasing a piece of silver paper in the wind - Alex Ferguson on Ryan Giggs

It's getting tickly now - squeaky-bum time, I call it – Alex Ferguson

If he was an inch taller, he'd be the best centre half in Britain. His father is 6ft 2in - I'd check the milkman – Alex Ferguson on Gary Neville

He's a novice - he should keep his opinions to Japanese football – Alex Ferguson on Arsene Wenger

It was a freakish incident. If I tried it 100 or a million times it couldn't happen again. If I could I would have carried on playing! – Alex Ferguson on the infamous boot incident with David Beckham

If Chelsea drop points, the cat's out in the open. And you know what cats are like - sometimes they don't come home – Alex Ferguson

I've never played for a draw in my life – Alex Ferguson

I don't like losing but I've mellowed. I maybe have a short fuse but it goes away quicker now – Alex Ferguson

If I was to listen to the number of times I've thrown teacups then we've gone through some crockery in this place. It's completely exaggerated, but I don't like people arguing back with me – Alex Ferguson

ZLATAN IBRAHIMOVIC

What can you say about Zlatan? Just ask Zlatan himself. He refers to himself in the third person and plays with the strength and skill of three people…..all of which are highly talented. That said, he is as daft as a brush.

I was like, no way, Zlatan doesn't do auditions. I thought you either know me or you don't and if you don't know me you can't really want me – Zlatan on the prospects of a trial with Arsenal in 2000

Only God knows... You're talking to him now – Zlatan

I don't think that you can score as spectacular a goal as those of Zlatan in a video game - even though these games are very realistic these days – Zlatan

What Carew does with a football, I can do with an orange – Zlatan

At Barca, players were banned from driving their sports cars to training. I thought this was ridiculous – it was no one's business what car I drive – so in April, before a match with Almeria, I drove my Ferrari Enzo to work. It caused a scene – Zlatan

First I went left, he did too. Then I went right, and he did too. Then I went left again, and he went to buy a hot dog – Zlatan

I didn't injure you on purpose, and you know that. If you accuse me again, I'll break both your legs, and that time it will be on purpose – Zlatan

Guardiola was staring at me and I lost it. I thought 'there is my enemy, scratching his bald head!'. I yelled to him: 'You have no balls!' and probably worse things than that – Zlatan

An injured Zlatan is a properly serious thing for any team – Zlatan

I'm not used to winning nothing – it's the first time it's happened to me. I'm disappointed. It's a failure – Zlatan

We are looking for an apartment; if we do not find anything, then we will just buy a hotel – Zlatan

I came like a hero, left like a legend – Zlatan

If I had played in England, I would have destroyed it, like I have everywhere else – Zlatan

I can't help but laugh at how perfect I am – Zlatan

Swedish style? No. Yugoslavian style? Of course not. It has to be Zlatan-style – Zlatan

When you buy me, you are buying a Ferrari. If you drive a Ferrari you put premium petrol in the tank, you hit the motorway and you step on the gas. [Pep] Guardiola filled up with diesel and took a spin in the countryside. He should have bought a Fiat – Zlatan

It's true I don't know much about the players here, but they definitely know who I am – Zlatan

Mourinho is Guardiola's opposite. If Mourinho brightens up the room, Guardiola pulls down the curtains – Zlatan

I won't be the King of Manchester; I will be the God of Manchester – Zlatan

I think I'm like wine. The older I get, the better I get – Zlatan

Who needs a nickname? To be afraid of me, just watch me play – Zlatan

It felt like I had 11 babies around me – Zlatan

ARSENE WENGER

Arsene Wenger led the famous Invincibles team at Arsenal in 2003/04 where the team were undefeated in the entire season. The fans loved him so much that they gave Arsene Wenger his very own hashtag for many years.......**#WengerOut**

I tried to watch the Tottenham match on television in my hotel yesterday, but I fell asleep - Arsene Wenger

A football team is like a beautiful woman. When you do not tell her, she forgets she is beautiful – Arsene Wenger

Of the nine red cards this season we probably deserved half of them – Arsene Wenger

I'm not a witch doctor, I'm just a football coach – Arsene Wenger

If you eat caviar every day it's difficult to return to sausages – Arsene Wenger

Everyone thinks they have the prettiest wife at home – Arsene Wenger

Ferguson's out of order. He has lost all sense of reality. He is going out looking for a confrontation, then asking the person he is confronting to apologise. He's pushed the cork in a bit far this time – Arsene Wenger

He's out of order, disconnected with reality and disrespectful. When you give success to stupid people, it makes them more stupid sometimes and not more intelligent – Arsene Wenger on his arch rival Jose Mourinho

The biggest things in life have been achieved by people who, at the start, we would have judged crazy. And yet if they had not had these crazy ideas the world would have been more stupid – Arsene Wenger

DIEGO MARADONA

Diego Maradona will forever be remembered throughout the world as one of the best footballers that ever lived. In England he will be mostly remembered for his "hand of God" goal that eventually dumped England out of the 1986 World Cup.

Messi scores a goal and celebrates. Cristiano scores a goal and poses like he's in a shampoo commercial – Diego Maradona

My legitimate kids are Dalma and Giannina. The rest are a product of my money and mistakes – Diego Maradona

I was waiting for my teammates to embrace me and no one came, ... I told them, 'Come hug me or the referee isn't going to allow it – Diego Maradona

My mother thinks I am the best. And I was raised to always believe what my mother tells me – Diego Maradona

If I could apologise and go back and change history I would do. But the goal is still a goal, Argentina became world champions and I was the best player in the world – Diego Maradona

Everybody in Argentina can remember the hand of God in the England match in the 1986 World Cup. Now, in my country, the hand of God has brought us an Argentinian pope – Diego Maradona

I hate everything that comes from the United States. I hate it with all my strength - Diego Maradona

There would be no debate about who was the best footballer the world had ever seen - me or Pele. Everyone would say me – Diego Maradona

You were only a goalkeeper – Diego Maradona

Pele should go back to the museum – Diego Maradona

GARY LINEKER

Golden Boot winner Gary Lineker has been an institution on UK TV screens for many years. His knowledge and experience of every flavour of potato crisp is unrivalled in the sporting world.

Soccer is a game for 22 people that run around, play the ball, and one referee who makes a slew of mistakes, and in the end, Germany always wins – Gary Lineker

There's no in between-you're either good or bad. We were in between – Gary Lineker

If somebody in the crowd spits at you, you've got to swallow it. – Gary Lineker

Chris Hughton has been sacked by Norwich. Now? With 5 games to go? Utterly bonkers! – Gary Lineker

I was quite good at football once, although other than that my speciality would be maths. I'm great at sudokus and find all the spin-off games pretty easy too - Gary Lineker

There is Twitter outrage at everything. Be it a pair of trousers or a short skirt, somebody, somewhere, will not like it – Gary Lineker

On TV, if you fluff your lines, nobody gives a toss. But if you fluff a penalty in the World Cup, well - we all know how much that matters – Gary Lineker

I hear it all the time in the street: 'It's the crisp bloke – Gary Lineker

I remember Nayim at Tottenham dived all over the place, and we used to say to him, 'What are you doing? – Gary Lineker

Basically, Walkers are putting real produce into their flavours, so the cheese and onion flavour is actually cheese and onion rather than just flavourings – Gary Lineker

SIR BOBBY ROBSON

Bobby Robson is best known as the England manager who guided England to a Quarter Final and Semi Final in successive World Cups. By all accounts he was one of the good guys but still gave us some classic funny quotes.

The first 90 minutes of the match are the most important – Bobby Robson

If you count your chickens before they've hatched, they won't lay an egg – Bobby Robson

We don't want our players to be monks. We want them to be better football players because a monk doesn't play football at this level – Bobby Robson

We've got nothing to lose, and there's no point losing this game – Bobby Robson

Alan Shearer has done very well for us, considering his age. We have introduced some movement into his game because he has got two good legs now. Last season he played with one leg – Bobby Robson

There is only one word to describe football and that is 'if only' – Bobby Robson

Titus looks like Tyson when he strips off in the dressing-room, except he doesn't bite and has a great tackle – Bobby Robson

There will be a game where somebody scores more than Brazil and that might be the game that they lose – Bobby Robson

Don't ask me what a typical Brazilian is because I don't know what a typical Brazilian is. But Romario was a typical Brazilian – Bobby Robson

Well we got nine and you can't score more than that – Bobby Robson

MARIO BALOTELLI

Super Mario! Quite possibly the maddest of all footballers in the world. And there is some competition for that title. He once burnt his house down after deciding to have a firework display in his bathroom.

Only Messi Is Better Than Me – Mario Balotelli

Mourinho is the best coach in the world, but as a man he still needs to learn manners and respect – Mario Balotelli

I don't celebrate because I'm only doing my job. When a postman delivers letters, does he celebrate? – Mario Balotelli

I am different - if you can find another like me, then I will buy you dinner! – Mario Balotelli

People who know me, love me. People who don't know me love me too... or they hate me – Mario Balotelli

I believe I am more intelligent than the average person – Mario Balotelli

When I lose my temper it's because I decide to. If I do something it's because I want to do it – Mario Balotelli

America is a great country. I've been in the south, in the centre and in the north. I like it. Americans are very good people. There's just too much air-conditioning – Mario Balotelli

Yes, I think I am a genius, but not a rebel – Mario Balotelli

I don't like golf. It's not for me, it's too quiet – Mario Balotelli

Rooney's good but not the best in Manchester – Mario Balotelli

ALLY MCCOIST

Ally McCoist is one of the faces of Scottish football and particularly Glasgow Rangers. One of the greats. He even won the Ballon D'Or in 1987…..the 21st place prize.

I'll play for Rangers as long as I can. Then spend the rest of my life being depressed – Ally McCoist

Not a massive fan of the vuvuzela I have to say – Ally McCoist

Some place I've got to say, absolutely beautiful. I can totally understand why Stalin had his summer Dacha down here – Ally McCoist

GIANLUCA VIALLI

Chelsea and Italian legend. It seems the madder they are, the more Italian they are. Must be something in the pasta.

David Moyes, in Italy, would have been sacked three times now – Gianluca Vialli

At the start of the season you're strong enough to win the Premiership and the European Cup, but you have to be as strong in March, when the fish are down – Gianluca Vialli

The only way to stop Thierry Henry? With a gun! – Gianluca Vialli

When Manchester United are at their best I am close to orgasm – Gianluca Vialli

If you make love every night you get bored – Gianluca Vialli

The referee was amusing. Here they either shoot you down with a machine gun or don't blow their whistle at all – Gianluca Vialli

You should take your time and do it now and again. Like watching football – Gianluca Vialli on making love

You should not do it every night – Gianluca Vialli on playing

football

GRAHAM TAYLOR

Graham Taylor was the manager of Watford and took them to Wembley with Elton John (for the FA Cup final not an Elton John concert). Became England manager and famously loved the long ball game. He did give us some memorable funny quotes though.

Very few of us have any idea whatsoever of what life is like living in a goldfish bowl, except, of course, for those of us who are goldfish – Graham Taylor

If it stays as it is, I can't see it altering – Graham Taylor

Being an ex-England manager, one that failed to qualify for the World Cup, is like being a dead politician – Graham Taylor

Napoleon wanted his generals to be lucky. I don't think he would have worked with me – Graham Taylor

Agents do nothing for the good of football. I'd like to see them lined up against a wall and machine-gunned. Some accountants and solicitors with them – Graham Taylor

The ambition of an England manager should be to become England manager – Graham Taylor

It was nothing personal: if it had been, I would have left him on so he could have suffered like everyone else – Graham Taylor

I'd never allow myself to let myself call myself a coward – Graham Taylor

Footballers are no different from human beings – Graham Taylor

Very few great goals actually go in – Graham Taylor

Shearer could be at 100% fitness, but not peak fitness – Graham Taylor

It's the only way we can lose, irrespective of the result – Graham Taylor

To be really happy, we must throw our hearts over the bar and hope that our bodies will follow – Graham Taylor

He's a player you only miss when he's not playing – Graham Taylor

Carlos Tevez's English should be better than what it is – Graham Taylor

The referee's got me the sack. Thank him ever so much for that won't you – Graham Taylor

Do I not like that – Graham Taylor

CHARLIE NICHOLAS

Charlie Nicholas was known as Champagne Charlie when he first arrived in London from Scotland. But his favourite tipple is now hilarious funny miss quotes. A stalwart on Sky Sports.

I've told you a million times, I don't exaggerate – Charlie Nicholas

What Newcastle lack is a lack of pace – Charlie Nicholas

Paul Jewell's sides are always hard to break down, although Manchester United have a habit of breaking his sides down pretty easily – Charlie Nicholas

I'm a strong believer that if you score goals, you win matches – Charlie Nicholas

Scottish football needs a kick in the arm – Charlie Nicholas

STAN COLLYMORE

Mercurial striker who could score spectacular goals from anywhere on the pitch. He could also say some spectacularly funny things too.

I faxed a transfer request to the club at the beginning of the week, but let me state that I don't want to leave Leicester – Stan Collymore

There were two female physios at the club. I spent a lot of time on the treatment table – Stan Collymore

One day, Geoff Thomas was moaning about something after training, so I got up and chinned him – Stan Collymore

Fernando Torres needs a new leash of life – Stan Collymore

Matty Jarvis had acres of time there – Stan Collymore

Sheikh Mansour is putting his money and his mouth where his mouth is – Stan Collymore

It's six of one, half a dozen of the other at least – Stan Collymore

The Bolton back four didn't have a cat on earth's chance – Stan Collymore

ALAN BRAZIL

Contrary to popular belief Alan Brazil isn't named after the World Cup winning country. He is from Scotland. He could win the World Cup for funny gaffes though.

In the papers this morning is police closing in on Ian Holloway….sorry…it's Palace closing in on Ian Holloway – Alan Brazil

There's a good-feel factor about Sheffield Wednesday – Alan Brazil

Levante have gone fourth in Serie A. If anyone can tell me what part of Italy Levante is in, please call. I've no idea – Alan Brazil

John Cross is feeling very boyish about Arsenal's chances – Alan Brazil

Scotland v Wales will be like a Cup tie – Alan Brazil

Tony Adams is braised for rejection from Arsenal – Alan Brazil

They gave the Serbian FA a poultry fine – Alan Brazil

Chelsea have to play Sunday night - the FA won't bulge – Alan Brazil

I saw Real Madrid the other day, against Gadaffi – Alan Brazil

I don't want to stir up a can of worms – Alan Brazil

I'm not going to single individuals out but Yakubu has missed loads of great chances – Alan Brazil

I've got my doubts, there's no doubt about it – Alan Brazil

I wouldn't touch Chimbonda with a barn door – Alan Brazil

The tackles are coming in thick and thin now – Alan Brazil

Clint Dempsey scored a last-minute winner to earn Tottenham a 1-1 draw against United – Alan Brazil

Paolo Di Canio is one picnic short of a hamper – Alan Brazil

ERIC CANTONA

The King of Manchester himself. Eric loved football so much that he would often like to show fans how to kick. Crystal Palace fans always appreciated it when he jumped into the stands to show them.

After his first training session in heaven, George Best, from the favourite right wing, turned the head of God who was filling in at left back – Eric Cantona

I am not a man, I am Cantona – Eric Cantona

My best moment? I have a lot of good moments but the one I prefer is when I kicked the hooligan – Eric Cantona

I'm so proud the fans still sing my name, but I fear tomorrow they will stop. I fear it because I love it. And everything you love, you fear you will lose – Eric Cantona

Deschamps gets by because he always gives 100 per cent, but he will never be anything more than a water carrier – Eric Cantona

When the seagulls follow the trawler, it's because they think sardines will be thrown into the sea. Thank you very much – Eric Cantona

Even as a footballer, I was always being creative – Eric Cantona

I didn't study; I live – Eric Cantona

I'm proud of what I achieved there, but a life built on memories is not much of a life – Eric Cantona

ROY KEANE

Notoriously shy and timid, Roy Keane was never one to get into a row or argument with anyone. He was renowned for his patience, courtesy and diplomacy.......actually I am thinking of someone else. Roy Keane was the complete opposite of everything I just said.

He's been like a fresh of breath air – Roy Keane

Aggression is what I do. I go to war. You don't contest football matches in a reasonable state of mind – Roy Keane

Away from home our fans are fantastic, I'd call them the hard-core fans. But at home they have a few drinks and probably the prawn sandwiches, and they don't realise what's going on out on the pitch – Roy Keane

The amount of fights I've had in Cork would probably be another book. I mean, people go on about my problems off the field, but they don't even know the half of it – Roy Keane

The last song before the players went on to the pitch was 'Dancing Queen' by Abba. What really worried me was that none of the players – not one – said: 'Get that s**t off.' They were going out to play a match, men versus men, testosterone levels were high. You've got to hit people at pace. F***g' 'Dancing Queen.' It worried me. I didn't have as many leaders as I thought – Roy Keane

Maybe Gary [Neville] deserves to be chased up a tunnel every now and then – there would be a queue for him, probably. But you have to draw a line eventually – Roy Keane

Will those on telly yesterday be remembered for what they've achieved? None whatsoever. I wouldn't trust them to walk my dog. There are ex-players and ex-referees being given air-time who I wouldn't listen to in a pub – Roy Keane

It's good to get angry. It's an emotion and part of the game. It's good to go a bit mad but I don't throw teacups around. That's not my style – I'd rather throw punches – Roy Keane

People say 'go with the flow' but do you know what goes with the flow? Dead fish – Roy Keane

Cloughie was dead right, absolutely. It was the best thing he ever did for me – Roy Keane on being punched by Brian Clough

People say I'm hard, I'm Mr Angry. I'm this, I'm that. I just want to win matches. There's no point going out there and being Mr Nice Guy – Roy Keane

I got Robbie's [Savage] mobile number and rang him. It went to his voicemail: 'Hi, it's Robbie – whazzup!' Like the Budweiser ad. I never called him back. I thought: 'I can't be f***** signing that – Roy Keane

Who do you think you are having meetings about me? You were

a crap player and you are a crap manager. The only reason I have any dealings with you is that somehow you are the manager of my country and you're not even Irish you English ****! – Roy Keane on Mick McCarthy

If they don't want to come because their wife wants to go shopping in London, it's a sad state of affairs. To me, that player is weak because his wife runs his life – Roy Keane

CHRIS KAMARA

We all love Chris "Kam" Kamara. If Cantona is the King of Manchester, Kam is King of gaffes. Pure comedy gold.

Berbatov put the penalty away like he was just putting a penalty away – Chris Kamara

Giroud scored a brilliant header with the last kick of the game – Chris Kamara

Is it still called Calcutta? I thought it was Bombay these days – Chris Kamara

Karl Henry's been sent off for a deliberate red card – Chris Kamara

The area you're trying to protect at corners is the goal – Chris Kamara

I don't really know what is happening Jeff – Chris Kamara reporting live from a match for Soccer Saturday, Sky TV

Barnsley have started off the way they mean to begin – Chris Kamara

Well done to the lady lineswoman – Chris Kamara

NIGEL GORDON-JOHNSON

Statistics are there to be broken – Chris Kamara

For Burnley to win they are going to have to score – Chris Kamara

Nicky Shorey is the provider but Shane Long has made this all on his own – Chris Kamara

Manchester City are defending like beavers – Chris Kamara

Alex McLeish has just had his hands in his head – Chris Kamara

PAUL MERSON

Paul Merson is an Arsenal Legend and still likes to have a run out playing football at a ripe old age. He is also a quarter Italian which may explain some of the following funny quotes.

There's only one person gets you sacked and that's the fans – Paul Merson

When Everton knock it long, they don't knock it long – Paul Merson

Reading won't have the confidence to be confident – Paul Merson

After Chelsea scored, Bolton epitulated – Paul Merson

Football's all about yesterday, it's all about now – Paul Merson

To fix the rut they will have to take two steps backwards to go one step forwards – Paul Merson

You can't bite your nose off to spite your face – Paul Merson

If you keep walking past the barbers, eventually you'll get a haircut – Paul Merson

**David Nugent tore up the Championship but he's gone to Ports-

mouth and he's a fish up a tree – Paul Merson

In England, Rooney is a world-class footballer in the world – Paul Merson

United won't fall asleep against Liverpool. They'll win it in their sleep – Paul Merson

I think Southampton will finish above teams that are well below them – Paul Merson

Every single player on the pitch is now in the Birmingham box, apart from two of them – Paul Merson

That shot moved like... I was going to say a shop, but the shop's shut – Paul Merson

Everton are literally a bag of Revells – Paul Merson

It's very difficult to play when your lung comes out of your air – Paul Merson

Ian Ashby is very underrated and it's right he gets the accolades he gets – Paul Merson

SAM ALLARDYCE

Sam Allardyce is known as Big Sam. Because he is big. He stands over 9 foot tall and is famous for the snow capped mountains on his head. He is also known for his big gaffes and hilarious quips.

Today was about our lack of ability to not produce the ability that we've got – Sam Allardyce

We couldn't defend a fish supper – Sam Allardyce

Hopefully Andy Carroll has only tweeted his hamstring – Sam Allardyce

We were not good enough today, particularly in the fringe department – Sam Allardyce

We played under the sort of pressure we've played under all season, albeit a different sort of pressure – Sam Allardyce

The only decisions I'm making at the moment are whether I have tea, coffee, toast or cornflakes in the morning – Sam Allardyce

I'm not going to make a present of Santa – Sam Allardyce

I squeezed into some very tight black pants and nailed the Moonwalk. I've even dressed up as Cheryl Cole – Sam Allardyce

I won't ever be going to a top-four club because I'm not called Allardici, just Allardyce – Sam Allardyce

The top clubs in England would not risk taking on me and my team. Nowadays they are rarely managed by anyone from Britain. They've got to get a fancy-dan foreigner in, it's almost compulsory – Sam Allardyce

Now we have another two weeks to wait to play our next game to let stupid football associations make money from friendlies – Sam Allardyce

GLENN HODDLE

Glenn Hoddle was one of England's classiest footballers. He took England to a World Cup and famously dropped Gazza. Not literally. That would be silly.

Getting picked gives you half that confidence, or 50 per cent of it – Glenn Hoddle

With all their guns flying, Tottenham would be a threat – Glenn Hoddle

There's a lot of work been put in that hasn't been put in – Glenn Hoddle

He is a goal scorer, not a natural born one - not yet. That takes time – Glenn Hoddle

He was a player that hasn't had to use his legs even when he was nineteen years of age because his first two yards were in his head – Glenn Hoddle

When a player gets to 30, so does his body – Glenn Hoddle

I didn't say them things that I said – Glenn Hoddle

I have a number of alternatives, and each one gives me some-

thing different – Glenn Hoddle

You can never compare two players that are different, they're never going to be the same – Glenn Hoddle

Arsenal haven't won anything for three years, so they're used to success – Glenn Hoddle

Michael Owen could be Sir Alex's best ever buy, even though he didn't buy him – Glenn Hoddle

Everton are now hitting the ropes running – Glenn Hoddle

There was nothing wrong with the performance, apart from throwing away the game – Glenn Hoddle

The FA Cup is still domestically the best cup in the world – Glenn Hoddle

I think in international football you have to be able to handle the ball – Glenn Hoddle

75% of what happens to Paul Gascoigne in his life is fiction – Glenn Hoddle

If anyone is found guilty, I will step on them – Glenn Hoddle

International football is one clog further up the football ladder – Glenn Hoddle

JACK CHARLTON

One of England's World Cup winning legends from 1966 and famous manager of the Republic of Ireland. He will be greatly missed for his great humour and even bigger character.

We probably got on better with the likes of Holland, Belgium, Norway and Sweden, some of whom are not even European – Jack Charlton

It was a game we should have won. We lost it because we thought we were going to win it. But then again, I thought that there was no way we were going to get a result there – Jack Charlton

Stay tight on Van Cleef – Jack Charlton telling Mick McCarthy to mark Lee Van Cleef. Unfortunately Lee Van Cleef was a Hollywood actor not playing for Holland at the time

Right…ghoulkeeper is the ghoulkeeper. Right back is the big laird, two centre-backs…the big laird and the big laird, left back, the little laird. Right wing…the big laird, centre mids…the two big lairds, left wide…the little laird, up front…the big laird and…'

Jack Charlton starts to click his fingers as he looked at George Reilly.

...and up front...erm...erm...erm...what's your name, son?' (Still clicking his fingers)

'You signed me yesterday from Watford for £200,000 . . . I'm George Reilly.'

'Aaah . . . is that your name? I always knew George Reilly as the big laird. – Jack Charlton announcing the team at Newcastle United

I wasn't very good at playing football. But I was very good at stopping other people playing football – Jack Charlton

Man United have shops all round the world. It's a big money spinner, plus the fact that they change their strip every five minutes – Jack Charlton

Soccer is a man's game, not an outing for mamby-pambies – Jack Charlton

I've seen them on television on a Sunday morning most days of the week – Jack Charlton

If in winning we only draw we would be fine – Jack Charlton

GARY NEVILLE

Gary Neville had an interesting managerial career. He was appointed manager of Valencia in Spain even though he spoke no Spanish. No problem, Gary perfected speaking English with a Spanish accent. Seemed to do the trick.

I can't stand Liverpool. I can't stand the people. I can't stand anything to do with them – Gary Neville

It was like he was being controlled by a 10 year-old on a PlayStation – Gary Neville

We're at the top of the cliff and we can either fall off the edge or keep climbing – Gary Neville

While we're living, the dreams we have as children, fade away'. Not if you support United – Gary Neville

It could end up like the Dog & Duck against the Red Lion – Gary Neville

Before games, the smell of burgers wafts down from the stands – Gary Neville

We always looked forward to playing Aston Villa to hear him mangle Ugo Ehiogu's name. "Make sure you pick up Ehugu, Ehogy, whatever his name is." – Gary Neville

The trouble with the transfer window is it creates a window where transfers have to be done – Gary Neville

If you don't like someone, don't shake their hand – Gary Neville

The rest of the Spice Girls wanted to invite the entire Bayern Munich team because they reckoned they'd never known blokes to be on top for 90 minutes and still come second – Gary Neville

He went in with his shuds stowing – Gary Neville

MICHAEL OWEN

Liverpool and England legend who scored one of the greatest World Cup goals against Argentina. Quick on the field but not so quick when it comes to commentary on the game.

It's a good run, but it's a poor run, if you know what I mean? – Michael Owen

Footballers these days often have to use their feet – Michael Owen

What a shot! That's completely unstoppable but the goalkeeper has got to do better for me – Michael Owen

He's elbowed him in the head, but there's nothing in it for me – Michael Owen

Alderweireld played really well last year for Tottenham, let's hope he can transfer that form to Spurs this season – Michael Owen

That would've been a goal had it gone inside the post – Michael Owen

Whichever team scores more goals usually wins – Michael Owen

That's a fantastic penalty, but he'll be gutted it went wide – Michael Owen

It's hit the facial part of his head, there – Michael Owen

When they don't score, they hardly ever win – Michael Owen

If there's a bit of rain about, it makes the surface wet – Michael Owen

When the ball is that still, it's wobbling in the air – Michael Owen

GRAEME SOUNESS

Liverpool hard man with a fantastic perm in his playing days. Unusually for a Scot he is quick tempered as often demonstrated with his disagreements with co commentators on TV.

With a body like he has, I want him to be a bully. But he is too nice - he is perfect son-in-law material, but I don't want a team of son-in-laws – Graeme Souness

Today's top players only want to play in London or for Manchester United. That's what happened when I tried to sign Alan Shearer and he went to Blackburn – Graeme Souness

Players who have more great games than other players are the great players – Graeme Souness

Without picking out anyone in particular. I thought Mark Wright was tremendous – Graeme Souness

Working with people on a field turns me on – Graeme Souness

Scottish football is full of hammer throwers – Graeme Souness

I won't be fining players for getting sent off – Graeme Souness

**Everton are a bigger club than Liverpool. Everywhere you go on

Merseyside you bump into Everton supporters – Graeme Souness

In my opinion, Man United had their trousers taken down paying £100 million – Graeme Souness on Paul Pogba's transfer fee

Paul Pogba, I see him dancing at a wedding, shooting hoops, and a cynic in me thinks he doesn't want to be at United. He doesn't wanna play for United. – Graeme Souness

If I'm sitting in Manchester United's dressing room today, I'm glad Romelu Lukaku has gone and don't want Paul Pogba in there with me either if he's not up for the fight ahead and is also keen to get away – Graeme Souness

RON ATKINSON

Big Ron Atkinson was the archetypal 70's football manager with big fur lined coat, perma-tan and lots of gold jewellery. We miss Ron and the fashion. And some of his great quotes.

I never comment on referees and I'm not going to break the habit of a lifetime for that prat – Ron Atkinson

Well, Clive, it's all about the two Ms - movement and positioning – Ron Atkinson

I'm going to make a prediction - it could go either way – Ron Atkinson

Carlton Palmer can trap the ball further than I can kick it – Ron Atkinson

Women should be in the kitchen, the discotheque and the boutique, but not in football – Ron Atkinson (Yikes!)

You can see the ball go past them, or the man, but you'll never see both man and ball go past at the same time. So, if the ball goes past, the man won't, or if the man goes past they'll take the ball – Ron Atkinson

There's nobody fitter at his age, except maybe Raquel Welch – Ron Atkinson

One of the reserves came up to me and said 'I'm finding it a bit hard, it's the first time I've ever been dropped'. So, I told him to do what Nick Faldo does and work at his game. Next thing I know he's doing exactly what Faldo does, he's taken up golf – Ron Atkinson

Well, either side could win it, or it could be a draw – Ron Atkinson

He dribbles a lot and the opposition don't like it - you can see it all over their faces – Ron Atkinson

I just wanted to give my players some technical advice. I told them the game had started – Ron Atkinson

For me their biggest threat is when they get into the attacking part of the field – Ron Atkinson

They've picked their heads up off the ground, and they now have a lot to carry on their shoulders – Ron Atkinson

They must go for it now as they have nothing to lose but the match – Ron Atkinson

All I do know is that I'll never be able to achieve what Tommy Docherty did, and that is take Aston Villa into the third division and Manchester United into the second division – Ron Atkinson

Their strength is their strength – Ron Atkinson

Now Manchester United are 2-1 down on aggregate, they are in a better position than when they started the game at 1-1 – Ron Atkinson

Someone in the England team will have to grab the ball by the horns – Ron Atkinson

How are they defensively, attacking-wise? – Ron Atkinson

Apart from picking the ball out of the net, he hasn't had to make a save – Ron Atkinson

He sliced the ball when he had it on a plate – Ron Atkinson

If you score against the Italians you deserve a goal – Ron Atkinson

Our fans have been branded with the same brush – Ron Atkinson

Moreano thought that the full back was gonna come up behind and give him one really hard – Ron Atkinson

I would not say he (David Ginola) is the best left-winger in the Premiership, but there are none better – Ron Atkinson

He'll take some pleasure from that, Brian Carey. He and Steve Bull have been having it off all afternoon – Ron Atkinson

He must be lightning slow – Ron Atkinson

The Spaniards have been reduced to aiming aimless balls into the box – Ron Atkinson

Woodcock would have scored but his shot was too perfect – Ron Atkinson

Scholes is very influential for England at international level – Ron Atkinson

They are playing above the ground – Ron Atkinson

Beckenbauer has really gambled all his eggs – Ron Atkinson

Liverpool will think 'we could have won this 2-2 – Ron Atkinson

That's not the type of header you want to see your defender make, with his hand – Ron Atkinson

ANDY GRAY

Andy Gray used to be the voice of football in the 1990's and 2000's. I have no idea why he isn't on TV anymore.

Can you believe that? A female linesman. Women don't know the offside rule – Andy Gray

(Oh yes....I am beginning to remember why now)

I don't like to see players tossed off needlessly – Andy Gray

People say footballers have terrible taste in music but I would dispute that. In the car at the moment I've got The Corrs, Cher, Phil Collins, Shania Twain and Rod Stewart – Andy Gray

If you don't hit the target, you're never gonna score – Andy Gray

I was saying the other day, how often the most vulnerable area for goalies is between their legs – Andy Gray

Carlos Tevez is so rich that when he retires he'll never have to play football again – Andy Gray

It's a lot harder to play football when you haven't got the ball – Andy Gray

**If you gave Arsene Wenger eleven players and told him to pick

his team, this would be it – Andy Gray

I was in Moldova airport and I went into the duty-free shop - and there wasn't a duty-free shop – Andy Gray

Anyone who takes drugs should be hammered – Andy Gray

My history's not very good, but did David win? – Andy Gray

KEVIN KEEGAN

Liverpool, Newcastle and England legend who wore his heart on his sleeve and had a perm that rivalled Graeme Souness. I once met Kevin Keegan at a hotel just outside of Southampton when he was manager of Manchester City. He came into the bar and asked if I had seen Nicolas Anelka anywhere. I said I had. I told him that Anelka was on a computer in reception. Kevin seemed quite depressed at the news and left.

Argentina won't be at Euro 2000 because they're from South America – Kevin Keegan

I'd love to be a mole on the wall in the Liverpool dressing room at half-time – Kevin Keegan

They're the second best team in the world, and there's no higher praise than that – Kevin Keegan

I had Micah Richards as a player at 16 and he was a man then. What is he now? A bigger man, probably – Kevin Keegan

The Germans only have one player under 22, and he's 23! – Kevin Keegan

I don't think there is anybody bigger or smaller than Maradona – Kevin Keegan

NIGEL GORDON-JOHNSON

I know what is around the corner - I just don't know where the corner is – Kevin Keegan

Even though two and two might look like four, it could be three or five – Kevin Keegan

England have the best fans in the world and Scotlands fans are second to none – Kevin Keegan

England have the best fans in the world and Scotland's fans are second to none – Kevin Keegan

I'm not disappointed - just disappointed – Kevin Keegan

In some ways, cramp is worse than having a broken leg – Kevin Keegan

A tremendous strike which hit the defender full on the arm and it nearly came off – Kevin Keegan

As a manager, you always have a gun to your head. It's a question of whether there is a bullet in the barrel – Kevin Keegan

You get bunches of players like you do bananas, though that is a bad comparison – Kevin Keegan

Over the course of a season, you'll get goals that are good disallowed and you'll get disallowed goals that are good – Kevin Keegan

You can't do better than go away from home and get a draw – Kevin Keegan

Picking the team isn't difficult, it's who to leave out – Kevin Keegan

Nicolas Anelka left Arsenal for £23 million and they built a training ground on him – Kevin Keegan

The ref was vertically 15 yards away – Kevin Keegan

Chile have three options - they could win or they could lose – Kevin Keegan

I came to Nantes two-years-ago and it's much the same today, except that it's totally different – Kevin Keegan

Batistuta is very good at pulling off defenders – Kevin Keegan

I've had an interest in racing all my life, or longer really – Kevin Keegan

I'll never play at Wembley again, unless I play at Wembley again – Kevin Keegan

I've kept really quiet, but I'll tell you something, he went down in my estimation when he said that. We have not resorted to that, but I'll tell you, you can tell him now if you're watching it, we're still fighting for this title, and he's got to go to Middlesbrough and get something, and... and... I'll tell you, honestly, I will love it if we beat them, love it! – Kevin Keegan

GEORGE BEST

Georgie Best was aptly named. One of the greatest footballers that has ever graced the world. He played as hard off the pitch as he did on it and seemed to have just the same amount of success.

If I had to choose between dribbling past 5 players and scoring from 40 yards at Anfield or shagging miss world, it'd be a hard choice. Thankfully, I've done both – George Best

I spent a lot of money on booze, birds and fast cars. The rest I just squandered – George Best

In 1969 I gave up women and alcohol - it was the worst 20 minutes of my life – George Best

Every team has a hard man. We had Nobby Stiles, Chelsea had Chopper, Arsenal had Peter Storey, Liverpool had Tommy Smith. Leeds had eleven of them – George Best

I used to go missing a lot... Miss Canada, Miss United Kingdom, Miss World – George Best

Pain is temporary, glory...lasts forever! – George Best

I never went out in the morning with the intention of getting drunk. It just happened – George Best

Pele called me the greatest footballer in the world. That is the ultimate salute to my life – George Best

He can't kick with his left foot, he can't head a ball, he can't tackle and he doesn't score many goals. Apart from that he's all right – George Best

I've stopped drinking, but only while I'm asleep – George Best

They told me I wouldn't make 25. Then it was 35, then 45. These were my doctors speaking - they're all dead now – George Best

If you make up your own mind, you can only blame yourself – George Best

People say I slept with seven miss worlds, I didn't. It was only four, I didn't turn up for the other three – George Best

I want to be remembered for my football and the pleasure I gave people – George Best

You can't trust very many people – George Best

I will respect this liver. After all, it's not mine – George Best

I was in for 10 hours and had 40 pints - beating my previous record by 20 minutes – George Best

To call Keegan a superstar is stretching a point – George Best

Even at the height of my fame, 50 per cent of the people who saw me wanted a fight; it's the downside of being a star player –

NIGEL GORDON-JOHNSON

George Best

Don't die like I did – George Best

ANDREA PIRLO

Andrea Pirlo is Italian so you should know by now that there will be some interesting quotes coming along. In 2006 the AC Milan Chairman wanted him to stay so much that he apparently gave him a blank cheque and asked Pirlo to fill in the number he wanted.

The only great English midfielder in my career was Paul Scholes. He had elegance in him. Others were pretenders – Andrea Pirlo

I don't feel pressure. I don't give a toss about it. I spent the afternoon of Sunday, July 9, 2006 in Berlin sleeping and playing the PlayStation. In the evening, I went out and won the World Cup – Andrea Pirlo

I lifted my eyes to the heavens and asked for help because if God exists, there's no way he's French – Andrea Pirlo

After the wheel, the best invention is the PlayStation – Andrea Pirlo

British teams bring me good luck – Andrea Pirlo

Roy Hodgson mispronounced my name. He called me Pirla (a term used in Milan dialect roughly translated as d***head), perhaps understanding my true nature more than the other managers – Andrea Pirlo

I thought about quitting because, after Istanbul, nothing made sense any more. The 2005 Champions League final simply suffocated me – Andrea Pirlo

To most people's minds, the reason we lost on penalties was Jerzy Dudek – that jackass of a dancer who took the mickey out of us by swaying about on his line and then rubbed salt into the wound by saving our spot kicks – Andrea Pirlo

You could see the red mist coming down and he just wasn't able to hide it. We could tell what was coming and so we'd commandeer all the knives. Gattuso would grab a fork and try to stick it in us – Andrea Pirlo

JOEY BARTON

Undoubtedly a talented footballer, Joey Barton also had a great talent for getting into one or two scrapes. Sent off 9 times and two stays at Her Majesty's pleasure, has made for a colourful career.

He couldn't put on a coaching session to save his life. I've spoken to people about him and he can barely lay out cones – Joey Barton

Sitting eating sushi in the city, incredibly chilled out reading Nietzsche – Joey Barton

My reputation will always precede me to the day I die. For some people, that probably can't be quickly enough – Joey Barton

Javier Pastore wouldn't get a beach ball off me if we were locked in a phone box. He's t*rd. Anyone who thinks he isn't is clueless – Joey Barton

How I wish the mass media had christened me Joe instead of Joey. I hate Joey, not going to lie. Nobody I respect calls me it – Joey (Joe) Barton

England did nothing in that World Cup, so why were they bringing books out? 'We got beat in the quarter-finals. I played like s**t. Here's my book.' – Joey Barton

Not arsed if they're Beckham's or not. £9.99 for a pair of gruds

from H&M is an outrage, do one Becks. They cost about 1p to make in a sweat shop in the Third World, is there no limit to what 'Brand Beckham' will endorse for a pound note? – Joey Barton

Neymar is like the Justin Bieber of football. Brilliant on the old YouTube. Cat p**s in reality – Joey Barton

Thiago Silva. That the same p**sy that's been injured all season. Another over-rated Brazilian. Sort your hamstrings out FatBoy – Joey Barton

VINNIE JONES

Before he was an international film star, Vinnie Jones was part of the Crazy Gang at Wimbledon FC. What they lacked in style and grace they made up for in physical contact. Just ask Gazza.

Winning doesn't really matter as long as you win – Vinnie Jones

Never underestimate the predictability of stupidity – Vinnie Jones

The FA have given me a pat on the back. I've taken violence off the terracing and onto the pitch – Vinnie Jones

My mum calls my temper 'Devilman.' They say you calm down with age, but I don't know. It never goes away – Vinnie Jones

I'd like to be the romantic lead one day, but I've got to grow my hair first – Vinnie Jones

I've always had my ear pierced with a diamond stud. I did it myself when I was 16 – Vinnie Jones

To me, England is past its sell-by date. It's not the country I grew up in – Vinnie Jones

**I got into moisturiser when I played football. If you're out in all

weathers you have to take care of your face – Vinnie Jones

All of my shows involve men in tights. It's a bit bizarre, really – Vinnie Jones

Egil Olsen should have gone six games ago. He was totally useless. I'd like to give him a right-hander! – Vinnie Jones

HARRY REDKNAPP

We all loved Harry Redknapp in the I'm a Celebrity jungle for his great stories. He was known as one of the proper old fashioned wheeler dealer managers. One of the great managers that England never had.

If you can't pass the ball properly, a bowl of pasta's not going to make that much difference! – Harry Redknapp

I left a couple of my foreigners out last week and they started talking in foreign. I knew they were saying "Blah, blah, blah, le b**tard manager..." – Harry Redknapp

Scholes was playing tiki-taka football when nobody in England knew what it was. He was another of those players, like Denis Law or Bobby Moore, who at 15 probably looked as if he wouldn't make it. Too small, you would think - can't run, dumpy little ginger nut - but then the ball would come to him and he would dazzle you. He was the best footballer in that Manchester United

midfield, better than Ryan Giggs and Roy Keane – Harry Redknapp

We've got sports scientists who insist it's important for the lads to eat after games to refuel, even if it's 2am. I used to refuel after games at West Ham until half past three in the morning in a different way - but then I'm old school – Harry Rednapp

I signed Marco Boogers off a video. He was a good player but a nutter. They didn't show that on the video – Harry Rednapp

It's like being on the Titanic and seeing there's only one lifeboat left – Harry Redknapp

Samassi Abou don't speak the English too good – Harry Rednapp

I write like a two-year-old and I can't spell – Harry Rednapp

I don't think there is any place in football for drinking. I have said on several occasions to players: You don't put diesel in a Ferrari – Harry Rednapp

Journalist: **'Have you received any death threats?'** Harry Redknapp: **'Only from the wife when I didn't do the washing up!'**

I hope that you have enjoyed this book just as much as I enjoyed writing it. If you laughed loudly enough to wake the elderly neighbours from their afternoon snooze, then please do head back to Amazon and leave a review to let everyone else know how much you enjoyed it.

If you didn't laugh out loud or even quietly to yourself then there is not much else I can do to help other than to give you one more funny quote from the greatest ever……

I think that France, Germany, Spain, Holland and England will join Brazil in the semi-finals – Pele

Thanks for reading!

BOOKS BY THIS AUTHOR

Find A Job In A Pandemic

Definitive guide to finding a job that destroys the myths of recruiting and shows you the behind the scenes tricks of the trade that will ensure that you get an interview and job offers when you most need them.

"This truly is a game changer"

Printed in Great Britain
by Amazon